Celebrate the Seasons
(Kindergarten)

**Written by
Carol Smith**

**Illustrated by
Vanessa Schwab**

**Cover Illustrated by
Kathryn Marlin**

All rights reserved—Printed in the U.S.A.
Copyright © 1999 Shining Star Publications
A Division of Frank Schaffer Publications, Inc.
23740 Hawthorne Blvd., Torrance, CA 90505

Notice! Pages may be reproduced for home or classroom use only, not for commercial resale. No part of this publication may be reproduced for storage in a retrieval system, or transmitted in any form or by any means—electronic, mechanical, recording, etc.—without the prior written permission of the publisher. Reproduction of these materials for an entire school or school system is strictly prohibited.

Unless otherwise indicated, the New International Version of the Bible was used in preparing the activities in this book. Scripture taken from the HOLY BIBLE, NEW INTERNATIONAL VERSION. Copyright © 1973, 1978, 1984 International Bible Society. Used by permission of Zondervan Bible Publishers.

Table of Contents

To Parents and Teachers 3

Spring (March–May)

Spring Nature Walk 4–5
Who Is My Mom? 6
"Eggs"tra Things to Do With Eggs ...7
Easter Festivities 8
Find the Palms 9
Palm Sunday 10
Mother's Day Treat.......................11
Mother's Day Cards......................12
Memorial Day 13
Grow Sprouts! 14

Summer (June–August)

Summer Fun!...............................15
Father's Day Treat........................16
A Card for Father.........................17
A Birthday Cake for America 18
John Hancock's Pen 19
Celebrate the Sun! 20
Drying Flowers 21
Planted Seeds 22
Labor Day Booklet...................23–25

Fall (September–November)

Autumn Nature Walk 26–27
Bird Feeders................................28
Fall Leaf Fun 29
Fallen Leaves Wall Hanging 30
Harvest Festival Ideas...................31
Pumpkin Snacks...........................32
Thanksgiving Festivities 33
A Thanksgiving Feast 34
Something Special 35

Winter (December–February)

Wonderful Winter.........................36
Tracks in the Snow 37
Christmas Hidden Picture 38
The Nativity Scene 39
Give a Gift 40
New Year's Celebration..................41
President's Day 42
Anonymous Valentines 43
Snowflake Fun.............................44

Which Is Which?................................45
Super Seasonal Fun 46
Clip and Copy Seasonal Art 47–48

© Shining Star Publications

SS48510

 To Parents and Teachers

Children love exploring the world around them. The activities in this book will help them focus on the everyday wonders and miracles of the four seasons God has given us. They'll enjoy observing, discovering, and learning about the many wonderful events that occur during each season of the year.

This book is filled with a wonderful variety of activities, including poems, songs, crafts, recipes, and so much more. While completing the stimulating activities, the children will be learning about God and His love for us and practicing such valuable skills as following directions, coloring, pasting, matching, drawing, writing, tracing, and finding hidden objects, among others.

Use the action rhymes and songs to familiar tunes to help children express their joy and excitement about what they've learned. Show them how to make simple crafts that they can take home as reminders of God's loving care for everything He made. Give them the student activity pages to help them learn to work independently. Encourage the children to pray with you, thanking God for the beauty of each season.

Most of the activities require easily-obtained materials, such as crayons, scissors, craft sticks, glue, etc. Some of the activities are intended to be outdoor experiences for the children. You may want to schedule some adult helpers on those days. Also included on pages 47 and 48 are wonderful pieces of clip art relating to the seasons. Use these for bulletin boards, invitations to seasonal events, special cards or pictures the children make, wall displays, parent communication, gift tags, and so much more.

Make the most of every idea and activity in this book to help children appreciate the seasons God gives us and the exciting differences they bring.

Spring Nature Walk

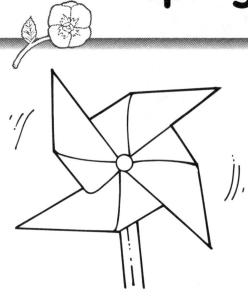

There is nothing quite like a nature walk in the spring! The grass is growing; flowers are starting to bloom; new life is apparent everywhere you look.

Plan ahead for a walk outdoors. Let the children make pinwheels (see directions below) to "see" the wind. Discuss shapes of clouds so the children know what to look for. Make some "trail mix" (see directions on page 5) to take along for a snack. You may want to take a rope for the children to hold onto so they can look around and yet not lose their way. Remind the children that God created everything they will see.

Scout out some locations where you can find new and unusual items. Here are some springtime things to look for: flower buds, flowers, clouds, butterflies, dandelions. (Add to this list some of your local springtime colors and plants.)

Try some of the activities below and on page 5 on your nature walk.
Note: You will want to make some preparations before the walk.

Perfectly Pretty Pinwheels

Help the children make pinwheels to take on their nature walk. To make a pinwheel pattern, draw two dotted lines and a circle in the center (see diagram to the right) on a 6" square piece of paper. Give each child a pinwheel pattern, a pushpin, scissors, and a pencil with an eraser. Have the children cut out the pattern on the dotted lines, stopping when they get to the circle. Show the children how to fold each corner into the center and fix it firmly into the pencil eraser by inserting the pushpin.

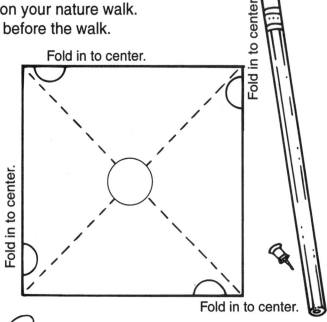

Watch the Clouds

Ask the Lord for rain in the springtime; it is the Lord who makes the storm clouds. He gives showers of rain to men, and plants of the field to everyone. (Zechariah 10:1)

Take some towels or blankets so that you and the children can watch the clouds and rest at the same time. Ask the children to find shapes in the clouds or to point out areas of the sky that particularly interest them.

Spring Nature Walk continued

Blow Bubbles

After you watch clouds for awhile, you may want to blow some bubbles. Mix together ½ cup of liquid dishwashing detergent (no additives like lemon scent), 1 ½ cups of water, and 1 cup of glycerin (check your local drugstore). For blowers, you can use toilet paper or paper towel tubes, bent coat hangers, slotted spoons, spatulas, or colanders. (Wave these bigger objects through the air rather than blowing on them.)

Dandy-Lion Ideas

Collect thistles for several different activities. Thistles are fun for children to blow. Explain to the children that by blowing on a thistle, they are helping distribute its seeds. Also, if you hold them tightly at the base between your thumb and forefinger, they are wonderful paintbrushes for a few strokes. Finally, if you take the flower or thistle off the stem, the stem is then a tube with one end larger than the other. This enables you to put the smaller end into the larger end to make a circle or to connect with other circles to make a chain or necklace.

Sketch a Springtime Scene

Let each child bring a sketchpad, a pencil, and crayons or markers outside and lay in the grass or sit on the sidewalk. Let the children sketch something they see that signifies spring.

Make Springtime Trail Mix

Mix pretzels, goldfish, popcorn, and raisins in a large bowl. Scoop a portion into a bag for each child to enjoy at a break on your walk, maybe when you're watching the clouds.

Who Is My Mom?

So many baby animals God created are born in the spring! Draw a line from each baby to its mother.

Aren't you glad God gave us mothers?

"Eggs"tra Things to Do With Eggs

Eggs are always popular in spring, particularly around Easter time. An egg symbolizes the beginning of new life. It has become not only food for us but a symbol of new beginnings as well. Try the activities below involving eggs.

Jigglin' Eggs
Materials:
4 packages of flavored gelatin, egg-shaped cookie cutters, 9" x 13" pan, spatula, apple juice, measuring cup

Directions:
You may want to prepare the gelatin outside of class by adding the four packages to 2¾ cups boiling apple juice and pouring it into the 9" x 13" pan to set for at least three hours. Then, just before class, dip the bottom of the pan in warm water for about 15 seconds. The children can then use the cookie cutters to cut the gelatin into shapes and the spatula to lift the shapes out of the pan. Fingers work fine for eating with this recipe.

Coloring Eggs
After boiling eggs, color them with crayons, with pellets you purchased at the grocery store, or with other foods. If you choose to use food, boil one of the following for three minutes: red cabbage, beets, orange peels, cranberries. Place the eggs in pots, cover them, and set them away from the heat for 20 minutes. These dyes will not be as bright as store-bought dyes, but they are fun for the children to try.

See-Through Egg
Create a "see-through egg" by soaking an uncooked egg in a full glass of vinegar overnight. The next morning, you can see right through the egg and even touch the membrane that encloses it. Let the children compare this to a boiled egg cut in half. Discuss the similarities and differences.

Easter Festivities

As you prepare for the Easter season, which is a big part of each Christian's spring, make your room into a mini Jerusalem. Below are some events you can highlight.

Jesus' Entry Into Jerusalem

Build a gate with paper or blocks around the entrance to your room. Make a "Welcome to Jerusalem" sign. (Matthew 21:1–11)

The Last Supper

This could include a table with some bread on a plate and a cup. As you tell the story, have someone sit at the table and show the bread and pour juice into the cup. (Luke 22:7–20)

The Cross on Which Jesus Was Crucified

You may have access to a cross that has been used in a previous display or celebration. If so, display it in another corner of your room. You may want to add a crown of thorns or a swatch of material. Use this setting when you tell the story of the crucifixion. (John 19:17–30)

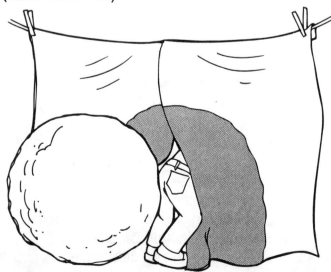

The Tomb in Which Jesus Was Resurrected

The empty tomb can be as simple as a large black circle on a wall, or it can be a "cave" made from a dark sheet that the children can walk into. You also can draw stone on brown paper to show the rock into which the tomb was carved. Use this setting when you teach about the resurrection. If you wish, you could also make a stone out of brown paper to cover the tomb with and then to roll away as you tell the story. (Matthew 28:1–10)

Find the Palms

One spring, people welcomed Jesus into Jerusalem by waving palm branches. Find the palm branches. Color them green. Look closely because some may surprise you!

Palm Sunday
Based on Matthew 21:1–11

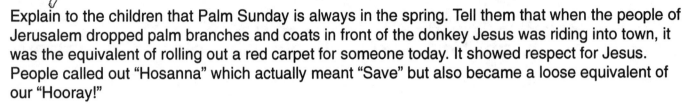

Explain to the children that Palm Sunday is always in the spring. Tell them that when the people of Jerusalem dropped palm branches and coats in front of the donkey Jesus was riding into town, it was the equivalent of rolling out a red carpet for someone today. It showed respect for Jesus. People called out "Hosanna" which actually meant "Save" but also became a loose equivalent of our "Hooray!"

Make a copy of the palm branch pattern below for each child. Re-enact Jesus' entry into Jerusalem by having the children lay the palm branches down at the entrance into your room. You may want to tape them down and leave them throughout the season as a reminder.

If you can work it out with your worship leaders, begin your worship service with the children and parents walking into the service waving their palm branches and calling out "Hosanna."

For More Fun:
Give each child a copy of the palm branch. Let the children color them, write their names on them, and glue them to the trunk of a large tree you draw on butcher paper. Let the children add flowers, butterflies, birds, etc., to the picture to create a springtime scene.

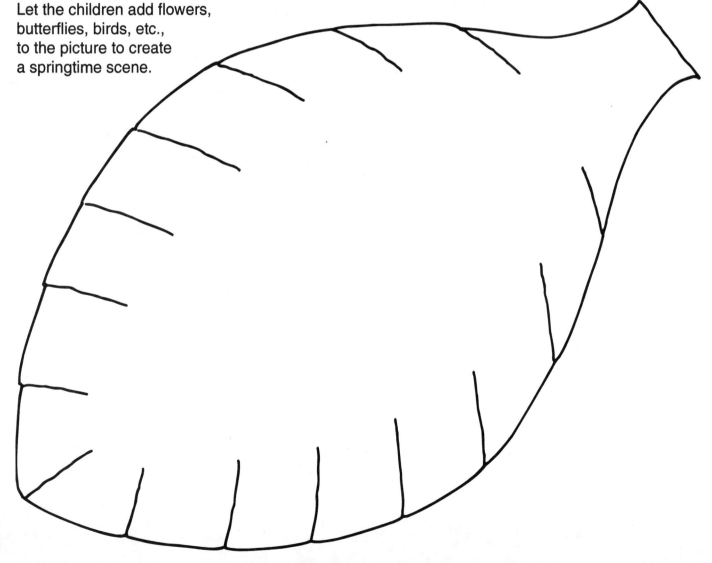

Mother's Day Treat

The Bible says *"Honor your father and your mother . . ."* (Exodus 20:12). Spring is a time to honor mothers. Mothers are very important to their children. Mother's Day is a time when we can show our mothers how much we love them. Let the children help you make the cookies below to give to their mothers as a special treat.

Note: Concerning Mother's Day and Father's Day, be sensitive to the children who are without one or both parents in their home. Talk with the children about the men and women in their lives who are special people to them, people who act like moms and dads. We can honor those people as well on these holidays.

Hungarian Butter Cookies

2 $\frac{3}{4}$ cups all-purpose flour
1 teaspoon baking powder
$\frac{2}{3}$ cup sugar
$\frac{1}{4}$ teaspoon salt
1 cup butter or margarine
1 egg
$\frac{1}{3}$ cup sour cream

Set the butter out the evening before. About two and a half hours before class, mix the dry ingredients in a large bowl. Add butter or margarine and blend with your hands until the mixture resembles coarse meal. Add egg and sour cream and mix until dough holds together. Cover and refrigerate about 2 hours.

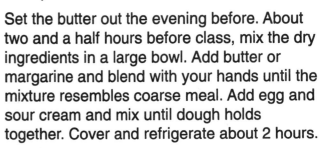

At the beginning of class, have the children wash their hands. Preheat oven to 350°. Give each child a pinch of the dough. Have the children form the dough into a ball and use their fingers to press it out to about a $\frac{1}{2}$" thickness. Then they can make crossmarks by pressing the back of a fork on top of each cookie. (Sturdy plastic forks will usually work.) Space the cookies out on a cookie sheet about 1" apart.

Bake for 20 minutes. Set aside to cool. By the end of class, the children can put the cookies in bags to take home for their mothers' special dessert.

Mother's Day Cards

Let the children make special springtime cards for their mothers. They are a perfect way for the children to tell their mothers how much they love them.

Fingerprint Cards

Materials:

ink pads of various colors, soap and paper towels for washing hands, construction paper, markers

Directions:

Before class, fold a sheet of construction paper in half for each child to form a card with a front cover and inside space for a message. Have the children write "Mom" on the fronts and "I love you!" on the inside of their cards.

A fun way to decorate the cards is to use fingerprints. Let the children press their fingers onto the ink pads and then put their fingerprints all over their cards. They can make designs with their prints or just randomly scatter them about. Remind the children that their cards are unique because each child's fingerprints are one-of-a-kind.

Flower Cards

Materials:

copies of the flower patterns, construction paper, glue, scissors, crayons or markers

Directions:

Give each child a sheet of construction paper and some of the flower patterns. Have each child fold his or her paper into fourths, like a card. The children can then decorate the fronts and backs of their cards with the flowers they color, cut out, and glue on. Help them write a special note to their mothers on the inside.

© Shining Star Publications

Memorial Day

On Memorial Day, we remember the people who died so that our lives could be better. Some of these people were soldiers who fought in wars so that we could live in our country and be free. Many cities and towns all over our country have parades to honor these special people.

Color the picture below. Trace and write "Thank you!" to honor the people who died.

Thank you!

Grow Sprouts!

When God made the earth, He also made everything plants need to grow: dirt, sunshine, and water. Let the children grow alfalfa sprouts in your classroom to learn how things grow. Remind them that many plants start growing in the spring.

Materials:
about two tablespoons of alfalfa seeds (from a health food store), quart glass jar, water, rubber band, measuring cup, cheesecloth or netting

Directions:

1. Put the seeds in a quart glass jar.

2. Put one cup of water in the jar.

3. Fasten cheesecloth or netting across the top of the jar with a rubber band.

4. Swish the water around in the jar to get the seeds all wet.

5. Put the jar with seeds and water somewhere dark overnight.

6. The next day, pour the water out through the netting over the jar.

7. For the next five days, pour water in the jar once a day, swish it around, and then pour it out through the netting. For these five days, leave the jar by the window.

8. After five days, your sprouts will be ready to eat on a salad or a sandwich or by themselves!

Summer Fun!

Put up big calendar pages of the summer months in your room. Each week, fill in the fun things the children did that week using the patterns below or others you create. You can put a child's name on a pattern and attach it to a particular calendar page. Add this verse to your calendar:

But may the righteous be glad and rejoice before God; may they be happy and joyful. (Psalm 68:3)

June

S	M	T	W	Th	F	S
					1	2
3	4	5	6	7	8	9
10	11	12	13	14	15	16
17	18	19	20	21	22	23
24	25	26	27	28	29	30

July

S	M	T	W	Th	F	S
1	2	3	4	5	6	7
8	9	10	11	12	13	14
15	16	17	18	19	20	21
22	23	24	25	26	27	28
29	30	31				

August

S	M	T	W	Th	F	S
			1	2	3	4
5	6	7	8	9	10	11
12	13	14	15	16	17	18
19	20	21	22	23	24	25
26	27	28	29	30	31	

Father's Day Treat

Summer is a time to honor fathers. Father's Day is the third Sunday in June. It is a day to remember "dear ole Dad." Below and on page 17 are ideas of things the children can make to honor their fathers. The Bible says *"Honor your father..."* (Exodus 20:12) Don't let the children forget to honor their Father in heaven on this day, too!

Special Note: Concerning Mother's Day and Father's Day, be sensitive to the children who are without one or both parents in their home. Talk with the children about the adult men and women in their lives who are special people to them, people who act like moms and dads. We can honor those people as well on these days.

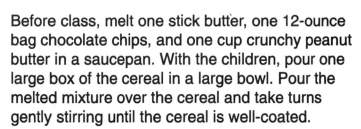

Daddy Chow

1 cup crunchy peanut butter, 1 large box crunchy rice cereal (like Chex™ or Crispix™), 1 stick butter, 1 12-ounce bag chocolate chips, 1 box confectioners' sugar, saucepan, spoon, large bowl, large paper grocery sack, resealable bags

Before class, melt one stick butter, one 12-ounce bag chocolate chips, and one cup crunchy peanut butter in a saucepan. With the children, pour one large box of the cereal in a large bowl. Pour the melted mixture over the cereal and take turns gently stirring until the cereal is well-coated.

Pour one box of confectioners' sugar into a large paper grocery sack. Pour the coated cereal into the sack, close tightly, and then let the children take turns shaking the bag. (This coats the cereal with the sugar and makes it a great finger food.) Divide the finished product into bags for the children to take to their fathers. (For the shaking part, you can divide the sugar and the cereal into two batches and two bags.)

A Card for Father

Don't let summer go by without letting the children honor their fathers on their special day. Let them make the cards below.

Materials:
butcher paper
yardstick
crayons and markers
decorative trims (rickrack, fabric scraps, ribbon, yarn, stickers, etc.)
glue
scissors
ribbon
tape

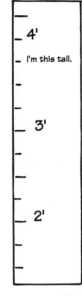

Directions:
Cut long strips of butcher paper (about 6" wide and long enough to be taller than the children in your group). Using a yardstick, mark off the inches and feet on the side of each paper strip, pretending it is a long ruler. Take turns taping the strips to the wall and measuring each child, marking his or her height by writing "I'm this tall!" Then lay the strips of paper on a table and let the children write the following down the length of the paper: "All of Me Wishes You a Happy Father's Day!" (You may need to help younger children with this.) The children can then decorate their strips any way they wish, using decorative trims, crayons, and markers.

Finally, fold the strips accordion-style until they are a manageable size for the children to carry and tie with ribbon to keep folded.

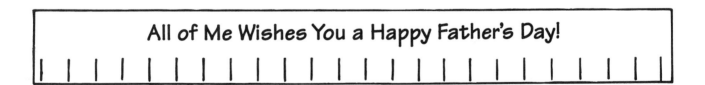

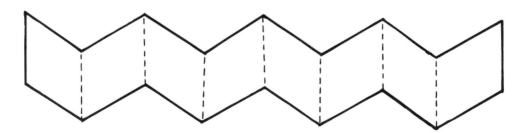

For More Fun:
Let the children use a large sheet of butcher paper to create a Happy Father's Day card for their Father in heaven.

A Birthday Cake for America

Explain to the children what the Fourth of July is. Ask them how they celebrate this special summer holiday. Then before class, make a cake in a 9" x 13" pan (any flavor you think the children will enjoy). With the cake, bring to class a large container of whipped topping, blueberries, strawberries, and birthday candles. Let the children use the whipped topping to ice the cake. Then they can use the strawberries to make the stripes (as on an American flag) and the blueberries to fill in the stars in the upper left-hand corner. Add the candles and put the cake in the refrigerator until you are ready to have a snack. Let the children sing "Happy Birthday" to America. Before eating, have the children thank God for giving us freedom and a wonderful country to live in. Then give them a copy of the birthday cake below to decorate for our country.

Color the cake. Trace and write "Happy Birthday U.S.A."

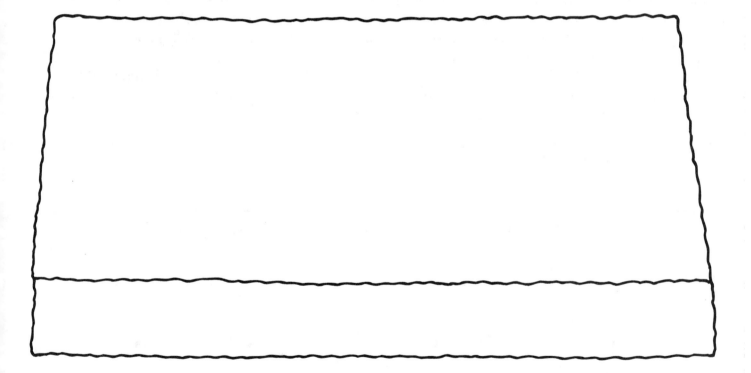

© Shining Star Publications
SS48510

John Hancock's Pen

Explain to the children that Independence Day is a time when we celebrate the day in the summer when men like John Hancock signed the Declaration of Independence. Tell them that this document told England that we wanted to be our own country, not just part of theirs. Being a free country, among many other things, means we can worship God any way we want to. Tell the children that pens used in those days were quill pens, made of feathers. We don't use those types of pens today, but we can make our pens look like them.

To do this, give each child a pen or pencil he or she can take home when the project is done. Then cut "feathers" out of construction paper by cutting triangles a little longer than the pens or pencils and about 2" at the widest point. Cut into the side to make fringe. Leaving enough room to hold the pen, tape the narrow end of the triangle around the pen or pencil so that the "feather" covers it.

Next, make your own document stating "We Are Glad to Live in Our Country!" Let the children sign their names to the document using their quill pens or pencils.

For More Fun:
Let the children make banners by tapping crepe paper strips to craft sticks. Then have a parade around the room. Teach the children the chorus of "The Battle Hymn of the Republic." Sing "Happy Birthday, America" and eat some cake and drink some red fruit punch!

Celebrate the Sun!

Let the children have fun celebrating the wonderful sun God gave us by trying the activities below.

Bible Verse Fun

Have the children memorize one or both of the Bible verses below. Or, have several children memorize parts of each and work together to say it. Be sure to discuss these verses with the children and let them illustrate them in pairs or groups on butcher paper.

The day is yours, and yours also the night; you established the sun and moon. It was you who set all boundaries of the earth; you made both summer and winter. (Psalm 74:16–17)

From the rising of the sun to the place where it sets, the name of the Lord is to be praised. (Psalm 113:3)

A Walk in the Sun

You will need blindfolds for half of the children for this activity. Take the children to a place that has both sunny and shady spots. Divide the children into pairs. Blindfold one partner of each pair and have the other partner lead him or her through the shady spots and the sunny spots. Have the blindfolded partners raise their hands whenever they feel they are in the sun. Let the partners take turns with the blindfold. Afterward, ask the children questions similar to the ones below.

- If you couldn't see, how did you know you were in the sun?
- Why do you think the sun makes us warm?
- Who created the sun?
- What would our world be like without the sun?

Make a Sunny Mural

Spread butcher paper along one wall of your room. In several places, write on the paper "Thank You, God, for the sun!"

Make paints of all kinds of sunny colors (bright yellow, orange, lime green, etc.) available to the children. Let them paint as many sizes and shapes of suns as they can imagine.

Drying Flowers

Jesus said: *"Consider how the lilies grow. They do not labor or spin. Yet I tell you, not even Solomon in all his splendor was dressed like one of these."* (Luke 12:27)

Drying flowers is a beautiful way to preserve nature and celebrate God's summer creation. While there are many ways to dry flowers, a simple and easy way for you to use with your children is to air dry them in your own space or in a dry storage room. Follow the directions below to create beautiful dried flower creations.

Materials:
flowers; a place to hang the flowers to dry for four to ten days (cool, dry, dark, with good circulation); string, elastic bands, or twine to tie the flowers together

Directions:
Gather your flowers together by their stems. Bunch them loosely enough so that air can still circulate around each flower. Keep in mind that grasses and ivies dry as well as flowers.

Hang the bunches, stems up, from the rafters of a shed or garage, on a nail, or from a broomstick hung horizontally across two props, such as chairs or beams.

Sunlight will lighten the color of the flowers, so if there are windows where the flowers are, make sure the sunlight doesn't fall across them.

Test for dryness after at least four days of hanging. Touch gently along the stem and bloom (if there is one). Everything should feel crisp. If the flower is not dried sufficiently, the neck of the flower will droop once you arrange it in an upright position. You may want to test a flower by placing it upright in a vase to see if the neck holds up. After drying, arrange the flowers or plants any way you like.

What to do with your dried flowers:
- Gather them into a bouquet with ribbon. Give them as a gift to cheer someone up.
- Leave the bunches hanging in your room all the way down one corner, from ceiling to floor.
- Use florist wire to stick the flowers in a foam base. Arrange them for a table setting. Or, stick them into a foam ball to hang them with a ribbon. (This is called a pomander and resembles a Christmas tree ball type of decoration.)
- Attach some flowers with florist wire to a vine wreath to make a wall hanging.
- Simply tie the stems of two bunches together with a ribbon (in a horizontal arrangement or an upside down "V") for an arrangement to hang over a door.

Planted Seeds

Summer is a time when things grow, grow, grow! Use your imagination to show what kind of plant might grow from this seed. It can be a plant that you've seen before or one that you create in your head. It can grow flowers or food. After you're finished, tell others all about your plant.

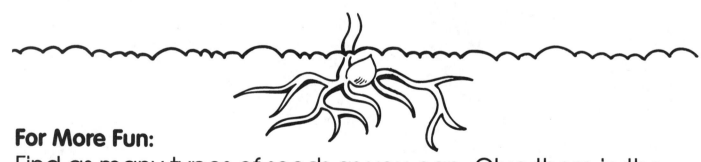

For More Fun:
Find as many types of seeds as you can. Glue them in the boxes.

Labor Day Booklet

Discuss Labor Day with the children before starting this activity. Explain to them that we have not always had the laws that we have now that protect workers and make sure they are treated fairly. Sing "I've Been Working on the Railroad" with the children.

Talk about what kinds of jobs people have. Let the children give suggestions, and give them time to think of as many different kinds of jobs as they can in preparation for the booklets they will be creating.

Let each child make a booklet. To do this, give each child a copy of the patterns below and on pages 24–25. Have the children cut out each page. Have the children name the occupation for

each page of the booklet. They can then color and accessorize each person according to his or her occupation. As you are explaining the activity to the children, review with them the verses at the bottom of each page. Children may then create covers for their booklets. After the covers are done, help the children put their pages in order with the covers on top and staple them down the left-hand side. The children can take the booklets home and share them with their families.

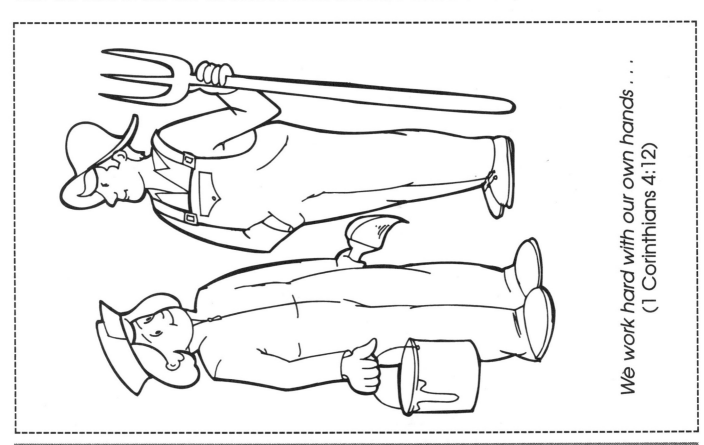

We work hard with our own hands.... (1 Corinthians 4:12)

Labor Day . . . continued

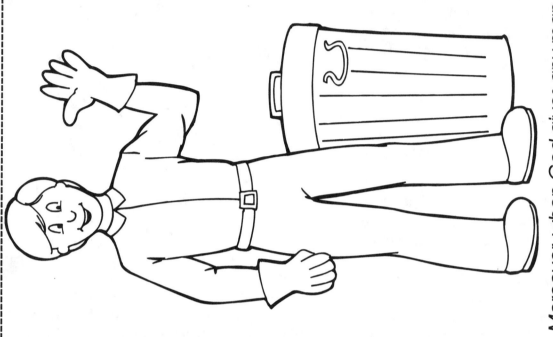

Moreover, when God gives any man wealth and possessions, and enables him to enjoy them, to accept his lot and be happy in his work—this is a gift of God. (Ecclesiastes 5:19)

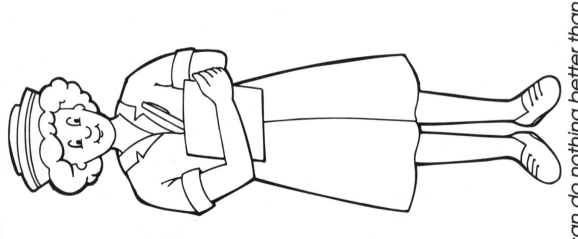

A man can do nothing better than to eat and drink and find satisfaction in his work. This too, I see, is from the hand of God. (Ecclesiastes 2:24)

Labor Day . . . continued

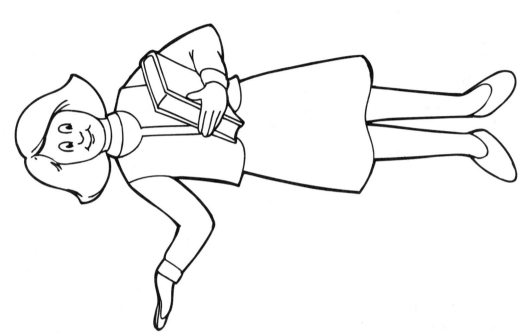

So I saw that there is nothing better for a man than to enjoy his work, because that is his lot. For who can bring him to see what will happen after him? (Ecclesiastes 3:22)

So I commend the enjoyment of life, because nothing is better for a man under the sun than to eat and drink and be glad. Then joy will accompany him in his work all the days of the life God has given him under the sun. (Ecclesiastes 8:15)

Autumn Nature Walk

Autumn is a fantastic time of year! Plan ahead for a nature walk in autumn. Prepare to collect a lot of leaves for in-class activities. Make some "Autumn Trail Mix" (page 27) with the children.

Scout out some locations where the children can find new and unusual autumn objects. Notice where the acorns and nuts are plentiful. Take some bags or baskets the children can use to collect leaves, pine cones, acorns, nuts, etc. There are many things you can do in class with these items. Try some of the projects below and on page 27.

Creative Fall Collages

After the children have collected a nice variety of items, give them large sheets of construction paper. Tell them to arrange their items creatively on the paper. They can make beautiful fall collages by gluing the items to their papers. Let each child share with the class what is included in his or her collage.

Fantastic Fall Mural

Draw a fall scene on a large sheet of butcher paper. Let the children glue real leaves to a tree you have drawn on it, acorns next to the leaves, etc. Title the mural, "Fantastic Fall."

© Shining Star Publications

Autumn . . . continued

Look for Tree Buds

As the rain and the snow come down from heaven, and do not return to it without watering the earth and making it bud and flourish, so that it yields seed for the sower and bread for the eater. (Isaiah 55:10)

Trees get their buds in the fall after their leaves are gone. This is the promise of spring. They are getting ready before the winter slumber. Have the children look for buds on branches. Have them draw a picture of what they saw when they return to class.

Watching the Ants

Ants are usually very active during the fall. They are making their colonies deeper to prepare for winter. They are collecting food to store. Take some sugar in a resealable plastic bag as you go on your walk and drop some around an ant colony. Let the children observe their behavior. Do they find the sugar? Do they go back and get the others? Tell the children about Bible verses that talk about ants collecting: *Ants are creatures of little strength, yet they store up their food in the summer.* (Proverbs 30:25)

Autumn Trail Mix

Mix pretzel sticks, dried fruit, candy-coated chocolates, nuts or seeds (such as sunflower or pumpkin), and raisins in a large bowl. Scoop a portion into a bag for each child to enjoy at a break on your walk, maybe when you're watching the ants.

After you watch the ants for a while, you may want to let the children blow some bubbles. If so, use the recipe found on page 5.

Bird Feeders

"Consider the ravens: They do not sow or reap, they have no storeroom or barn; yet God feeds them. And how much more valuable you are than birds!" (Luke 12:24)

There are many things God has given the birds in nature to feed on: seeds, nuts, berries, acorns. Sometimes, though, it is nice to help God take care of the birds. Make some bird feeders with your children by following the directions below. Before beginning the activity, prepare a place in your room to hang the bird feeders until it is time to take them home.

Materials:
peanut butter
pine cones
birdseed in a couple of sizes
   in a bin several inches deep
string (cut in 2" lengths)
plastic knives and spoons
resealable plastic bags

Directions:
With the help of a volunteer, have each child tie a string around the top of a pine cone so that it can be suspended with the stem pointing down. After the string is attached, allow the children to fill their pine cones as much as possible with peanut butter. They don't need to cover them with peanut butter, they just need to fill the crevices. A knife or the back of a spoon works well for this. For younger children, you may want to put the peanut butter on the utensil or even in the crevices and then let them pack it in.

After the peanut butter is packed in, let the children roll their pine cones in the seed bin. They should use their fingers to pack the seeds into the peanut butter, trying to cover them so much that they can't even see them.

When the pine cone bird feeders are covered well, slip them in the plastic bags with the strings hanging out of the bags. Seal the bags around the string and hang the feeders until it is time to take them home.

Use the remaining seed to fill more permanent bird feeders that can be viewed from your room so that you can watch the birds until spring.

© Shining Star Publications   SS48510

Fall Leaf Fun

Fall is a really fun time of year. The weather changes, leaves change color, and many other changes occur. Help the children make fall leaves following the directions below.

Materials:
crayons
9" x 12" sheets of oaktag
one copy of the leaf pattern below, enlarged on a 9" x 12" sheet of paper per child
stapler
green construction paper
scissors

Directions:
1. Give each child a piece of oaktag. Have the children color them with beautiful fall colors of orange, red, yellow, and brown. Tell each child to blend these colors and to cover the entire sheet.

2. Give each child an enlarged copy of the leaf pattern. Have each child cut out the leaf pattern without cutting through the edge of the paper. To do this, show the child how to pinch the leaf in the middle and make a cut big enough for the scissors to fit in.

3. Then have the child cut out the leaf and discard it. All the children need is the paper and leaf outline.

4. Staple the sheet with the leaf outline to the colored oaktag on three sides. Do not staple the stem side. The leaf will have beautiful fall colors.

5. Cut the green construction paper to a size to fit inside and behind the leaf outline.

6. Show the children how to slowly slide the green paper between the leaf outline and the oaktag to show how leaves change color.

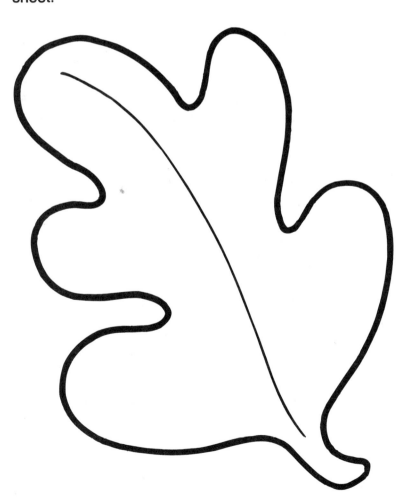

© Shining Star Publications

SS48510

Fallen Leaves Wall Hanging

Either collect fallen leaves for this wall hanging activity or use the leaves you collected on your nature walk (page 26). (Construction paper leaves will also work.)

Materials:
waxed paper, colored leaves (dry to the touch), an iron, scissors, pen, hole punch, string or twine, leaf patterns below and on page 29 (optional), construction paper (optional), ribbon or garland type decorations, glue (optional)

Directions:
Let each child choose several leaves for his or her window hanging. If you don't have the opportunity to collect leaves, use the patterns to cut out your own leaves from construction paper. Have the children place their leaves carefully on the waxed paper. (You might need to help younger children. For older children, you may want to tape the corners of the waxed paper to the table while they are working.)

After the leaves are placed, cover them with another sheet of waxed paper. With the iron on the warm setting, lightly iron the waxed paper until it melts together.

To decorate further, use a pen to draw a circle around each leaf. Let the children cut around the circles. (This will also make the waxed paper uniform without having to match the sides exactly as you iron.) Punch a hole at the top of each circle and tie twine, string, or ribbon through it.

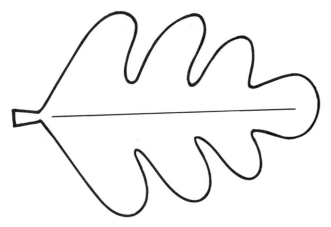

If the children enjoy art activities, you may want to let them decorate their window hangings with borders of ribbon or glitter. If not, they are ready to hang in the window.

The children could make window hangings to take home and then make some larger ones together for your classroom. You can also make strips of leaf collages to use as bulletin board borders.

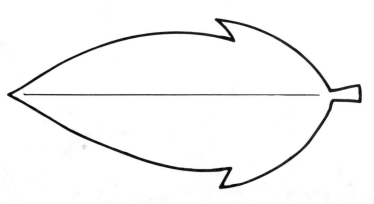

Harvest Festival Ideas

If you like to provide your group of children with an alternative to trick-or-treating, try some of the activities below.

Dress Up and Give to Others

Let the children dress up in non-scary costumes and visit a retirement or rest home. You can even make outfits together by asking them to wear clothes that can get dirty (jeans, oversized shirts, and baseball hats) and using makeup to dress them up as clowns (red noses and big smiles) or bullies (black eyes and smudged faces).

Give the children treats to give to the retirement home residents, such as travel-sized bottles of lotion. Afterward, have a party of your own at which the children receive treats.

Cookie Time

Bring in fall-shaped cookies (leaves, pumpkins, apples, etc.), icing, and sprinkles. Let the children decorate some cookies to eat and some to give away. The children can make some for another class, for sick friends, for the principal, etc.

Festival Fun

See if the parents are willing to help create an old-fashioned fall festival. Parents could set up activities like bobbing for apples, a pumpkin carving contest, a cake walk, pumpkin beanbag toss, and other fun games. Serve hotdogs, caramel apples, popcorn balls, and apple cider.

Costume Crazy

Provide the children with all kinds of materials (fabric scraps, old clothing, grocery sacks, markers, crayons, glue, ribbon, etc.) they can use to create costumes to resemble their favorite Bible characters. Let each child give clues to the other children about who he or she is. Let each child give the other children a treat when his or her identity has been determined.

Pumpkin Snacks

The snacks below are fun for the children to help you make to celebrate fall. Discuss with the children their favorite things God has made that you see in the fall as they eat these treats.

Pumpkin Seeds

If you have used a pumpkin in your classroom for any other activities, save the seeds from the pulp. If not, bring in a pumpkin to cut open. Scoop the seeds and pulp out onto newspaper and let the children "harvest" the seeds. Wash the harvested seeds in a colander, then follow this simple recipe for a yummy snack!

Preheat oven to 250°. In a large shallow pan, combine these ingredients:

    2 tablespoons vegetable oil
    ½ teaspoon salt
    ½ teaspoon Worcestershire™ sauce
    pumpkin seeds

Mix all ingredients together. Then put them in the oven to dry for 30 minutes. (If possible, you may want to stir lightly every 10–15 minutes.) If you have plenty of pumpkin seeds, you may want to dry some (no seasoning) on the windowsill to add to bird feeders outside. Talk about the miracle of seeds, God's way of making things continue to grow year after year.

Pumpkin Bread

Make pumpkin bread with the children, or bake it ahead of time and let the children ice it. Note: It is delicious, too, without icing!

Combine and beat the following:

    2 cups sugar
    2 cups flour
    3 teaspoons cinnamon
    1 teaspoon salt
    2 teaspoons baking soda
    1 cup vegetable oil
    1½ cups pumpkin
    4 eggs

Icing (optional):
1 pound powdered sugar
1 stick butter
8 ounces cream cheese
2 teaspoons vanilla
1 cup nuts (optional)

This recipe makes two loaves. Bake at 350° for 50–55 minutes.

Thanksgiving Festivities

Use any or all of the activities below and on page 34 to celebrate Thanksgiving with the children. Some of them are just plain fun, and some help the children practice having thankful hearts. While Thanksgiving is easily associated with turkeys, pilgrims, and pumpkin pie, it is also a command from God for our lives. We please Him with a celebration of thanksgiving any day throughout the year.

I will praise God's name in song and glorify him with thanksgiving.
(Psalm 69:30)

Enter his gates with thanksgiving and his courts with praise; give thanks to him and praise his name.
(Psalm 100:4)

A Turkey Hunt

Before class, hide paper turkeys all over the room and send the children around to find them. This will help "get the wiggles out." (A pattern is included to the right for your use.) Be sure to count how many you hide so that you will know when all have been found. Make sure all turkeys are found and emphasize this to the children. Tell the children "The Parable of the Lost Sheep" (Luke 15:1–7) and relate this to finding all the turkeys. Tell the children that each of us is important to God.

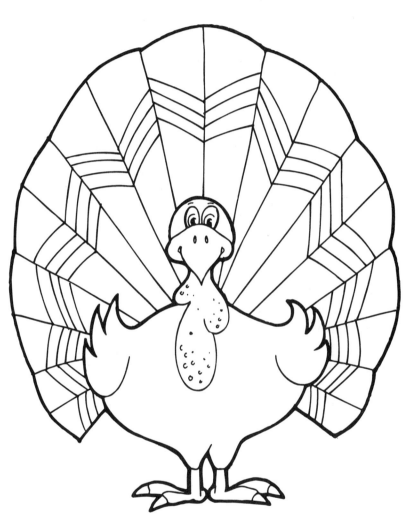

Super Thankful Songs

Sing together some songs thanking God. Try the ones below.

Thank You, Lord
(Tune: "Allelujah")

Lord, we thank You.
Lord, we thank You.
Lord, we thank You.
Lord, we thank You.
Lord, we thank You.
Lord, we thank You.

Number One
(Tune: "Row, Row, Row Your Boat")

Thank You, Thank You, Lord,
For all that You have done,
For all that You have given us,
Dear Lord, You're Number One!

© Shining Star Publications   SS48510

A Thanksgiving Feast

Children love Thanksgiving feasts. Let the children help you plan one to have in your room before Thanksgiving break. Try some of the ideas below or use some of your own.

Thank You, God, Place Mats
Provide the children with magazines, scissors, glue, and large sheets of construction paper. Help each child write, "Thank You, God, for the food You give us," on a large sheet of construction paper. Then tell the children to cut out pictures of foods for which they are thankful and paste them all over their papers. Laminate the place mats and let the children use them at their feasts.

Thankful Napkin Holders
Give each child copies of the patterns below to create napkin holders for their classroom feast and for their families to use on Thanksgiving. Have the children color them and glue them to strips of construction paper. Then they glue each strip to create a circle that they can slip over a paper napkin.

Fancy Feast Ideas
Communicate with parents to plan the Thanksgiving feast. Try to include turkey, corn, mashed potatoes, cranberry sauce, pumpkin pie (see recipe below), and any other items the children feel are necessary. The children can use their place mats and napkin holders. Have them memorize the prayer below to say before eating their feast.

We thank You, Lord,
For the food we eat.
We thank You, Lord,
For bread and meat.

We thank You, Lord,
For all You do.
Help us love You
Each day through.

A Perfect Pumpkin Pie
This recipe is for a no-bake pumpkin pie! Make it with the children and eat it in the same hour. At the beginning of the hour, mix together the following: 1 can of pumpkin pie mix (not just pumpkin pie, but the mix that is already sweetened and has spices in it), 1 large container of whipped topping, 8 ounces of cream cheese (room temperature).

Let the children help stir. Fill two graham cracker crusts, letting the children help smooth out the filling. Put them in a refrigerator or ice chest until you are ready to serve.

Something Special

Color in every space that has the number "3" in it. What have you made? Color the spaces around it using many bright colors. This will remind you to be thankful all the time, not just on Thanksgiving!

Wonderful Winter

Winter is a great time of year! Christians celebrate the birth of baby Jesus and Epiphany—the celebration of the wise men's visit to Jesus. Try some of the activities below to get the children involved in this special season and in these special celebrations.

Christmas Picture Books
These books are a wonderful way for the children to learn the Christmas story.

Materials:
old religious Christmas cards; 9" x 12" sheets of paper; glue; yarn, stapler, or brads

Directions:
Assemble a book of plain paper for each child. Bind it with yarn, staples, or brads. The children will select Christmas cards of their choice to glue on each page to depict the Christmas story. The children may then dictate or write the text for their books. When complete, send the books home so the children can share the wonderful story of Christmas with their families.

Heavenly Angels

Materials:
white and other colors of construction paper, multicultural flesh-colored paper, glue, markers, scissors

Directions:
Trace circle heads on the flesh-colored paper. Trace triangle bodies on the colored paper. Have the children cut these out. Trace both of each child's hands on the white paper for wings and cut them out. Have the children glue the heads to the points of the triangle bodies and glue the wings coming out from the back. Let each child use markers to add a face (an oval for the mouth makes it look as if the angel is singing) and decorate the body. Display the angels on a bulletin board entitled "Hark! The Herald Angels Sing!" After the children have made these angels, tell the children the story of the shepherds (Luke 2:8–20).

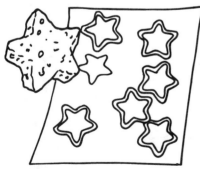

Shining Stars
This activity is fun for the children to do. Discuss with the children the bright star the wise men followed to find baby Jesus (Matthew 2:1–12).

Materials:
dark blue or black paper, white paint, trays, glow-in-the-dark paint, star-shaped sponges, paintbrush

Directions:
Have the children use the star-shaped sponges dipped in white paint to print stars on their paper. When dry, use the glow-in-the-dark paint to outline a few stars on each child's paper. Let dry. The glow-in-the-dark paint needs to be exposed to light for one minute. Then the children can take their papers to a dark place and watch the stars shine!

© Shining Star Publications

Tracks in the Snow

Winter is a time when many animals rest. God created animals with special abilities for survival. Animals almost never get lost. Many find their way home using their strong sense of smell.

Can you follow these tracks to the animals' homes? Use different colors of crayons to trace each animal's trip home.

Christmas Hidden Picture

Based on Luke 2:1–20

How many stars and angels can you find in this picture? Some are easy to see, but some are hidden. Do you know what stars and angels have to do with the story of Jesus' birth?

stars _____

angels _____

The Nativity Scene

Different countries celebrate Christmas in different ways. In France, Christmas is called Noël. There, decorating the Christmas tree is not the main family activity; setting up the Nativity scene is. If you have a Nativity scene for your room, make its arrival a festivity. Let the children take part and make it a big event. You may even want to build a small crèche or stable (big enough for the children to fit into) and have the children act out a live nativity scene for several weeks preceding Christmas. Copy the nativity scene below for children to color and cut out. Show them how to fold where indicated to make it stand.

Give a Gift

Christmas cookies make wonderful gifts for some senior citizens. Buy some refrigerated cookie dough that comes in a roll. Cut the roll into round slices and let the children help you make angels, snowmen, and Christmas tree cookies using the round slices to make someone's winter a cheery one!

The children can decorate the cookies with sprinkles before baking or with colored frosting after baking. Deliver them singing the chorus to "The First Noël."

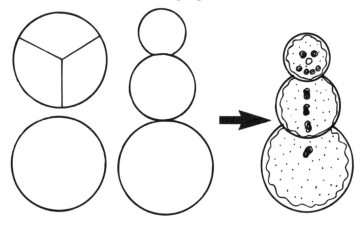

Snowman

Use two round pieces. One round makes the lower body. Cut ⅓ of another round to roll out to make the head. Use the remaining ⅔ to roll out to make the middle.

Angels

Use three round pieces for two angels. One round makes the body and wings (cut the wings of each side and invert them). The other round makes the other body, and the third round splits in half and rolls out to make the heads.

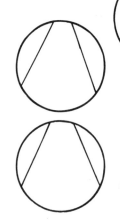

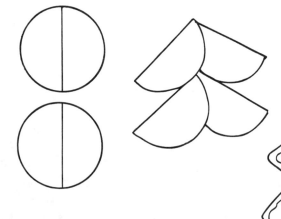

Tree

Use two round pieces. Cut both round pieces in half and place the rounded sides together to make the boughs of a tree. As the cookie bakes, the tree blends together.

For More Fun:

Let the children fold pieces of paper into fourths and cut out snowflake designs. They can put these in with the cookies.

New Year's Celebration

New Year's Day is the only holiday celebrated in almost every country, even if not on the same day. The Chinese celebrate it for 15 days in January or February. Try some of the activities below to get the children excited about this special winter holiday.

Merry Messages

Tell the children that in Belgium, children write their parents New Year's messages on decorated paper. Ask the children what message they would like to write to their parents. Come up with a universal message. Help the children decorate paper and write their message on it to give to their parents.

Make Some Wassail!

Wassail is a drink traditionally served on New Year's Eve and Day. There are many recipes for Wassail. This is a simple one you might want to use in your class:

- large container of apple juice or cider
- 2 sticks of cinnamon
- 1 lemon, sliced thinly lengthwise
- 1 orange, sliced thinly

Heat the cinnamon and cider to boiling, then simmer for 15 minutes. Add orange and lemon just before serving. If it is too warm, add an ice cube to each cup as you serve it. (If you have a picky group, just use apple juice.)

Read a New Year's Poem Together

Read the poem below, having the children chime in on "Happy New Year!"

We're all at the beginning,
And that is why you hear:
Happy New Year!
Happy New Year!

We're hoping for some good things.
We don't have much to fear,
Happy New Year!
Happy New Year!

We know that God will lead us.
We know He'll keep us near.
Happy New Year!
Happy New Year!

We all are here together,
And so we give this cheer:
Happy New Year!
Happy New Year!

New Year's Resolutions

Discuss New Year's resolutions with the children. Make a class list of resolutions the children can make in order to be better and stronger Christians.

President's Day

Everyone must submit himself to the governing authorities, for there is no authority except that which God has established. The authorities that exist have been established by God. (Romans 13:1)

President's Day is a day in the winter when we honor the leader and past leaders of our country. The children can try the activities below to learn more about the U.S. presidents.

Presidential Prayer

On President's Day, have a special time of prayer for the leaders of our country. Write a short note to the President letting him know that you prayed for him. Let the children sign it. Address it to Mr. President, The White House, 1600 Pennsylvania Avenue, Washington, D.C., 20500.

Draw a Picture

Give each child a copy of the frame below. Have the children draw a picture in the frame of what they would do if they were president. Display the pictures in the hall and then include them in your packet to the President.

Anonymous Valentines

When valentines first became a custom, they were sent anonymously. Make some valentines and decide with your class who to send them to anonymously. Some options include a senior citizen's group, a "special kids" class, parents, and staff members.

Give the children different colors of paper, folded in half, and copies of the heart patterns on this page to make the valentines. The children can use the hearts to decorate the fronts of the cards. Inside, the children can write some of the verses below or choose some of their own messages to use.

I thank my God every time I remember you. (Philippians 1:3)

It is right for me to feel this way about . . . you, since I have you in my heart. (Philippians 1:7)

Keep yourselves in God's love as you wait for the mercy of our Lord Jesus Christ to bring you to eternal life. (Jude 1:21)

And so we know and rely on the love God has for us. God is love. Whoever lives in love lives in God, and God in him. (1 John 4:16)

Other Messages:

I love you!!!

You're my valentine!

You are loved!

Snowflake Fun

Snowflakes are a fun part of winter. God often covers the earth in a cold blanket of white snow. Make your own snowflake following the directions below.

Materials:
two 8" white paper plates, hole punch, sharp scissors, dark blue crayon, silver glitter, glue, white thread, large sheet of paper, snowflake patterns on this page

Directions:
1. Trace around snowflake pattern 1 onto the center of a paper plate and cut it out. Discard the cutout pattern.

2. Trace around pattern 2 onto the center of the other paper plate and cut it out.

3. Using a paper punch, make holes where indicated on the small loose snowflake (pattern 2).

4. Punch a hole above the cutout pattern 1 on the paper plate. Tie a short length of thread between pattern 2 and the plate, allowing pattern 2 to swing freely.

5. Using a dark blue crayon, print neatly around the border of the plate:
   . . . wash me, and I will be whiter than snow. (Psalm 51:7)

6. Apply glue at various places on the snowflake and sprinkle glitter over the glue. Gently shake off excess glitter.

7. Attach another length of thread at the top for a hanger.

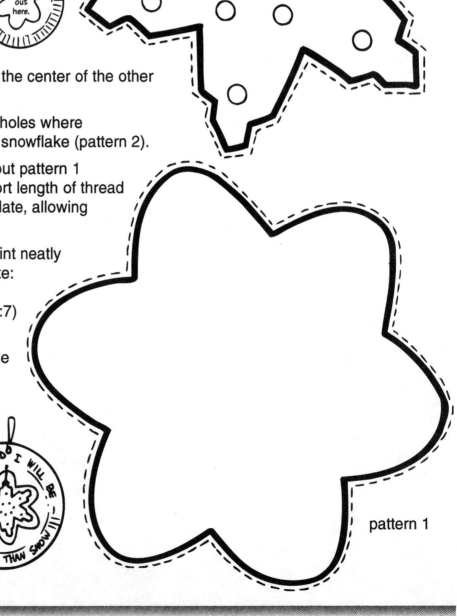

Which Is Which?

And God said, "Let there be lights in the expanse of the sky to separate the day from the night, and let them serve as signs to mark seasons and days and years." (Genesis 1:14)

Each of the four seasons God created is special. Each one has its own special qualities. Color each picture according to the name of the season it belongs to.

Spring—pink   Summer—red   Fall—brown   Winter—blue

Super Seasonal Fun

Below are some fun ways the children can demonstrate their knowledge of the seasons.

Draw the Seasons

Give each child four pieces of paper. Have the children draw one season on each page. Next, help them tape the pages together and fold them to make an accordion mural that can be looked at, one page at a time, or unfolded to be spread out on a table or a wall.

Nature Collages

Give each child a large sheet of paper. Have the children divide their papers into four sections. Each section should be labeled with one of the seasons. Have the children find items to glue in each section to represent each season. The children can use items found outside, crayons, markers, fabric scraps, pictures from magazines, etc., to create their collages. Let each child tell the class what he or she is most thankful for in each season. (Note: This is a good group project, too.)

Seasonal Treats

Divide the children into four groups. Assign each one a season. Help each group plan or prepare a treat that is appropriate for its particular season. Let the groups share their treats with each other.

Guess the Season

Let each child choose an activity to pantomime relating to one of the seasons. Let the other children try to guess what the season is.

Season Day

Each day for four days, let the children bring in or wear clothing for a particular season. Have them also bring in, or you can serve, food and drinks relating to the season of the day.

Clip and Copy Seasonal Art

Clip and Copy Seasonal Art